"F" Is for Families

by Annalisa McMorrow
illustrated by Marilynn G. Barr

Dedicated with love to G.G. and Jack.

Publisher: Roberta Suid
Design & Production: Standing Watch Productions
Cover Design: David Hale

P.O. Box 1680
Palo Alto, CA 94302

E-mail us at: MMBooks@aol.com
Visit our Web site: www.mondaymorningbooks.com

ISBN 1-57612-152-6

Printed in the United States of America
987654321

Contents

Introduction

Understanding family history is a good way to introduce students to the concept of studying the past. *F Is for Families* is a month-long unit filled with informative and exciting cross-curriculum activities. Family-related history, language, math, art, spelling, homework, and game activities are featured for each week. Songs are also included.

Use the "Family Tree" (p. 6) to introduce the unit. This sheet uses several Family Trees to focus on relationships within families. It also introduces the concepts of relatives and ancestors. Then help children make their Family Portfolios. They can use these to store all of their family-related activities in the classroom, or to take materials home to share with their own families.

Patterns throughout the unit can serve many purposes. For instance, duplicate the leaf patterns from "Planting a Family Tree" for use as name tags, or desk or cubby labels, or enlarge patterns to use as bulletin board decorations.

The activities in *F Is for Families* are intended for grades one through three. Some lessons may easily be simplified for younger children. For instance, if children cannot write their own reports or stories, they can dictate them to the teacher or teacher's helper, record them on a tape recorder for an audio report, or draw pictures to represent the words.

Graphic organizers accompany several language activities. These forms help the children to stay focused on the topics that they are researching or learning about.

The unit ends with a final game that allows children to share the knowledge that they've learned over the four weeks' of study. Once children have finished the game, give the students Genealogist Diplomas (p. 64), to show that they have mastered the concept of family relationships.

To extend the *F Is for Families* unit, look for family-related books to store in your reading corner, such as the *Ramona* series by Beverly Cleary, the *Alexander* series by Judith Viorst, or the *Tales of a Fourth Grade Nothing* series by Judy Blume. Many books for children deal with a wide assortment of styles of families. Even the popular Harry Potter books mention the family that he lives with—although it's not a very pleasant one. Challenge children to be on the lookout for mentions of families in books and magazines that they read on their own.

If possible, invite children's family members to visit the classroom during this unit. Grandparents make great interview subjects, and younger brothers and sisters will be thrilled to be included in any family-themed activity.

The Web is a good place to locate information, especially about ancestors, family names, and family history. Remember, Web sites change with frequency. Always check sites yourself before sharing them with the students. Below are several nonfiction books for teachers' use. Share facts and pictures with your students. Also listed are children's books for students to read on their own and chapter books about families to read to the classroom.

Family-related Books:

- *A Bargain for Frances* by Russell Hoban (Harper & Row)
- *Barrio: Jose's Neighborhood* by George Ancona (Harcourt Brace)
- *Bunny Money* by Rosemary Wells (Dial)
- *How My Family Lives in America* by Susan Kuklin (Simon & Schuster)
- *A Kurdish Family* by Karen O'Connor (Lerner)
- *Ramona Quimby, Age 8* by Beverly Cleary (William Morrow)
- *The Runaway Bunny* by Margaret Wise Brown (Harper & Row)
- *Superfudge* by Judy Blume (Dutton)

Family Tree

Families come in many different forms. In this family tree, the most recent generation is shown at the bottom. The ancestors are shown at the top. Branches show the generations in between. Maternal is someone related to the mother. Paternal is someone related to the father.

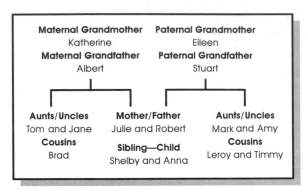

Maternal Grandmother	Paternal Grandmother
Katherine	Eileen
Maternal Grandfather	**Paternal Grandfather**
Albert	Stuart

Aunts/Uncles	**Mother/Father**	**Aunts/Uncles**
Tom and Jane	Julie and Robert	Mark and Amy
Cousins	**Sibling—Child**	**Cousins**
Brad	Shelby and Anna	Leroy and Timmy

Other family trees might look very different. For instance, here are several based on famous stories.

The Three Little Bear's Family Tree

Mama Bear ———— Papa Bear

Baby Bear

The Old Woman Who Lived in a Shoe's Family Tree

Old Woman

Child Child Child Child Child Child

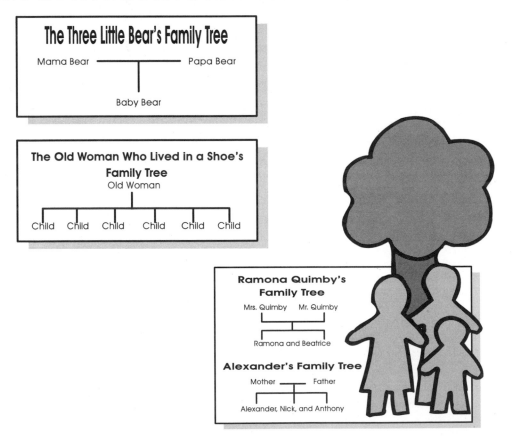

Ramona Quimby's Family Tree

Mrs. Quimby   Mr. Quimby

Ramona and Beatrice

Alexander's Family Tree

Mother ———— Father

Alexander, Nick, and Anthony

You can create a family tree for many characters that you read about!

F Is for Families © 2002 Monday Morning Books

Family Portfolio

Materials:
Portfolio Patterns (p. 8), scissors, crayons or markers, glue, hole punch, yarn, legal-sized folders or large sheets of heavy construction paper

Preparation:
Duplicate a copy of the Portfolio Patterns for each child.

Directions:
1. Demonstrate how to make a portfolio. If using legal-sized folders, punch holes along the two open sides. Cut two arm-length pieces of yarn and tie knots in one side of each. Thread the yarn through the holes and tie the free ends together to make a strap. If using construction paper, fold the paper in half to make a folder, and then continue as described above.
2. Give each child a sheet of patterns to color and cut out.
3. Have the children decorate their portfolios with the patterns.

Options:
• The children can add their own hand-drawn pictures, as well. Or they can cut out pictures from magazines to glue to their portfolios.
• Cover the portfolios with contact paper for added sturdiness. Reinforce the holes with hole reinforcers.

Portfolio Patterns

F Is for Families © 2002 Monday Morning Books

Interview a Family Member

This activity allows children to develop their interviewing skills by questioning a member of their immediate family.

Materials:
Interview Organizer (p. 10), pens or pencils, *The Stupids Step Out* by Harry Allard

Preparation:
Duplicate a copy of the graphic organizer for each child.

Directions:
1. Read *The Stupids Step Out* to the children.
2. Explain that the children will be writing their own short stories about a funny experience that their family had. However, they will first need to do some research by interviewing a family member.
3. Give each child a graphic organizer. Let the children practice interviewing each other in the classroom ahead of time. They can ask each other the questions on the sheet, without writing in the answers.
4. Have the children take the sheets home to fill in by interviewing family members.
5. Ask the children to bring the completed sheets back to the classroom on a specific day.

Option:
Younger children can take the organizers home, as well. A parent or guardian can help read the questions and then write the answers.

The silliest story I remember about my family is when...

Interview Organizer

My name is: _____

I am interviewing: _____

Relation to me: _____

1. What is the silliest story you remember about our family?

_____

_____

_____

_____

2. When did it happen?

_____

_____

3. How old were you when it happened?

_____

_____

4. Did you think it was silly at the time? If not, when did you realize that it was silly?

_____

_____

_____

_____

5. Would you change the event if you could? If so, how?

_____

F Is for Families © 2002 Monday Morning Books

Silly Stories

Children can use the interviews that they did previously for this activity. Or they can share a silly anecdote that they personally remember about their own families. Consider sharing a story from your own family history to start the activity.

Materials:
Filled-in organizers (p. 10), paper, pens or pencils, crayons or markers

Preparation:
None

Directions:
1. Have the children write very short stories describing silly experiences. They can use the ones retold by a relative, or choose one they remember from their own lives.
2. The children can illustrate their short stories using crayons or markers.
3. Give each child an opportunity to share his or her story with the rest of the class. Then bind the stories into a classroom *Silly Story Book,* or post the stories on a bulletin board.

Options:
• Younger children can dictate their stories.
• Place children's books that feature silly family stories near the children's work. For instance: *Alexander and the Terrible, Horrible, No Good, Very Bad Day* by Judith Viorst; *The Day Jimmy's Boa Ate the Wash* by Trinka Hakes Noble; *You're the Scaredy Cat* by Mercer Mayer; *Tales of a Fourth Grade Nothing* by Judy Blume, or any of the books in the *Ramona* series by Beverly Cleary.

When I was three years old ...

How Many Toys?

This math activity can be used for different levels of mathematical study. For younger children, write a plus sign in the ball in the middle of each equation. Write in a multiplication sign for older children.

Materials:
Counting Toys (p. 13), pencils, crayons or markers

Preparation:
1. Fill in the missing signs (+ or x), then duplicate the Counting Toys pages. Make one for each child.
2. Make an answer key for self-checking, if desired.

Directions:
1. Give each child a copy of the Counting Toys sheet.
2. Have the children do the problems. They count the toys on the left side of the equation and then add or multiply the number of toys by the numeral written on the right side of the equation. They draw the correct number of toys in the answer box or write in the correct numeral.
3. Children can share their answers with the class. Or they can use the answer key for self-checking.

Options:
• For older children, white out the numeral and write in larger numerals for more advanced math study.

Counting Toys

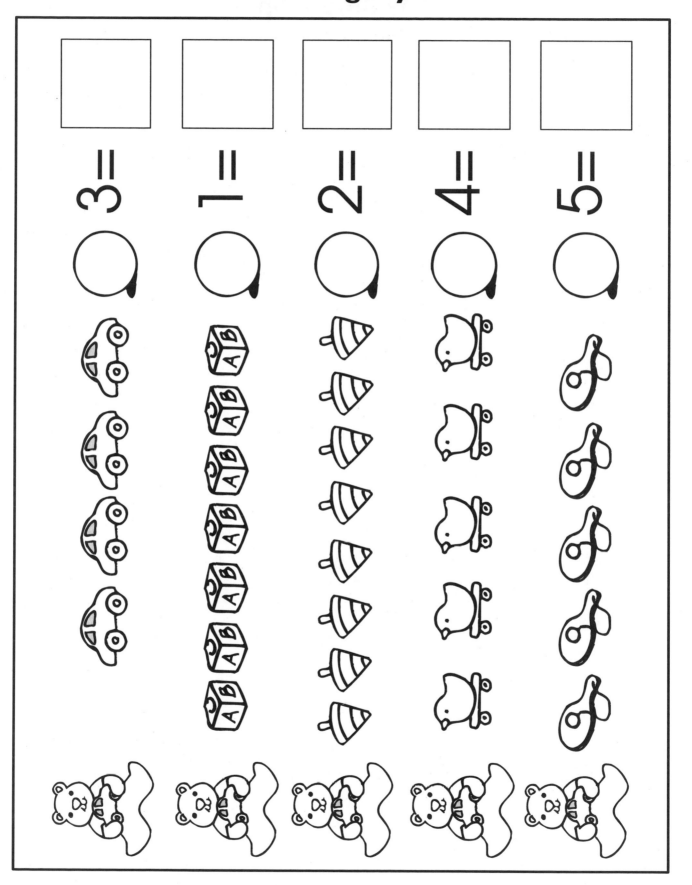

Family Album Spelling

Materials:
Family Frames (p. 15), Family Album (p. 16), bag, construction paper, scissors, colored markers

Preparation:
1. Duplicate a copy of the Family Frames for each child and one for teacher use.
2. Cut the frames apart and color as desired.
3. Enlarge the album pattern and post on a bulletin board.

Directions:
1. Announce a date for a spelling "bee."
2. Divide the students into small groups. Have the children work together to learn the words. Let the children take the Family Frames home to study.
3. On the day of the spelling bee, put the frames in a bag. Pull one frame from the bag at a time and have a child spell the word on the frame.
4. If the child spells the word correctly, he or she can post the frame in the album. If not, another child tries to spell the word.
5. Continue until each child has a chance to spell one word and all of the frames are posted on the board.

Options:
• Re-use words to let each child have a turn.
• White-out the given spelling words and write in other family-related words, including: relative, niece, nephew, grandson, granddaughter, baby, sibling, mother-in-law, and so on.

F Is for Families © 2002 Monday Morning Books

Family Frames

Family Album

Family Portrait

These personal portraits make perfect gifts for holidays, or have the children use them as gifts for Mother's Day, Father's Day, or Grandparents' Day

Materials:
Drawing paper, crayons or markers, pencils, construction paper, scissors, glue

Preparation:
None

Directions:
1. Give each child a sheet of drawing paper, and explain that the children will be drawing pictures of their families.
2. Children can sketch their drawings first using pencils. Or they can draw with crayons or markers from the start.
3. Once the pictures are finished, demonstrate for the children how to make construction paper frames. Fold a large piece of colored construction paper in half and cut a rectangle from the center. The remaining paper becomes the frame.
4. Children can glue the frames to their pictures.
5. Display the pictures in the room and invite the parents for a gallery opening.

Options:
• Help the children write each family member's name on the portrait or frame.
• Show children pictures of portraits by famous artists before doing this activity.

Family Concentration

Materials:
Family Frames (p. 15), crayons or markers, scissors, clear contact paper

Preparation:
1. For each game, make two copies of the Family Frames.
2. Color as desired, cover with clear contact paper for protection, and cut out.

Directions:
1. To play the game, the players turn all of the cards face down. Then they take turns flipping two cards over. If the pictures on the cards match, they keep both and try again. If the cards don't match, they turn them face down and another child takes a turn.
2. The children can take the concentration game home to play with their families.

Option:
Older children can practice spelling the names of the different family members ("mother," "grandfather," and so on) as they turn over the cards.

Family Member Songs

There Are Moms and Dad
(to the tune of "Do Your Ears Hang Low?")

There are moms and dads.
There are grandmas and grandpas.
There are aunts and uncles, too.
There are nieces and nephews.
It would surely be a shame
If all families looked the same!
Wouldn't that be sad?

My Family is Made Up of People
(to the tune of "My Bonnie Lies Over the Ocean")

My family is made up of people
Who all are related to me.
Nobody's family is just like mine.
I have my own great family!

Playing with Names

Materials:
The Name Game (p. 21), paper, pencils

Preparation:
Duplicate a copy of The Name Game sheet for each child.

Directions:
1. Have the children take home the Name Game sheet.
2. The children can work with family members to see how many words they can create using the letters of their names.
3. Consider playing this game in the classroom ahead of time using the letters in your name, or in the name of a favorite storybook character, such as Alexander from *Alexander and the Terrible, Horrible, No Good, Very Bad Day*. For example:

```
Alexander
    a
    an
    and
    den
    red
    ear
    land
    led
    lead
    lean
    learn
    leader
```

Note:
Younger children can use only their first names for this game. They can count words that are single letters, such as "a" or "I." Older children can make up words using other family members names, as well.

The Name Game

Write down your first, middle, and last name:

_____

Write the words you can spell using the letters in your name:

_____

_____

_____

_____

_____

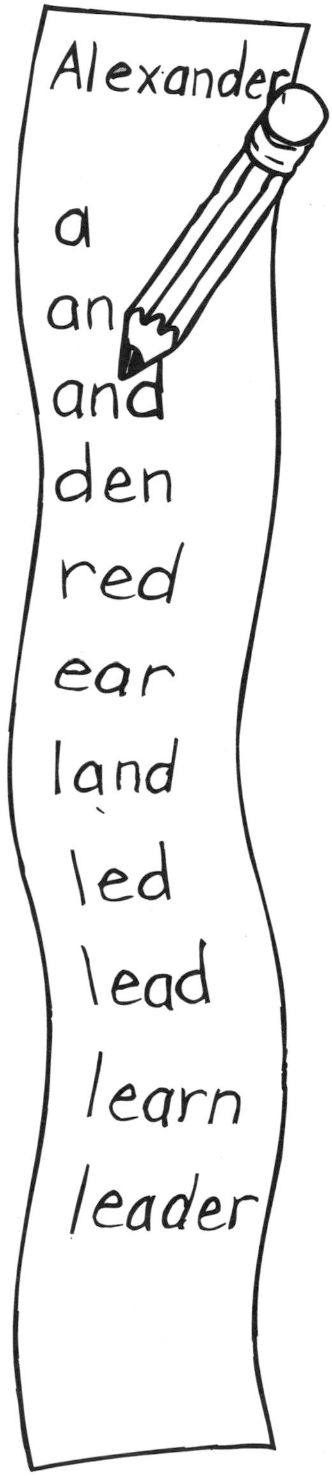

Write your favorite storybook character's name:

_____

_____

Write the words you can spell using the letters in the character's name:

_____

_____

_____

_____

_____

Alexander

a
an
and
den
red
ear
land
led
lead
learn
leader

Planting a Family Tree

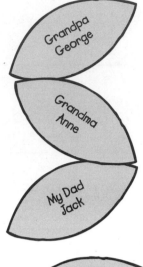

This activity allows children to create a memorable family tree of their own.

Materials:
Family Tree (p. 23) Leaves (p. 24), colored construction paper, crayons or markers, drawing paper, scissors, hole punch, yarn or brads

Preparation:
Duplicate the Leaves and the Tree patterns for each child.

Directions:
1. Explain that the children will be making their own family trees. Send the patterns home with the children.
2. Have the children work with their families to make the trees. They will be cutting out the leaves and gluing them to the trees. Each leaf will represent a different family member. Younger children might only include their parents and siblings. Older children might include aunts, uncles, cousins, grandparents, and so on.
3. Have the children bring the finished family trees back to school. Post them on a bulletin board, or gather them in a classroom album.

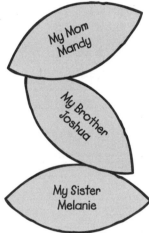

Options:
• If posting the patterns on a bulletin board, consider adding a real leaf border.
• Children can add drawings or photographs to their trees.

F Is for Families © 2002 Monday Morning Books

Family Tree

Leaves

Creating a Newspaper

Children will write about important events that took place during the lifetime of one of their relatives. This writing activity gives children the chance to practice their research skills.

Materials:
Paper, encyclopedias or other resources, pens or pencils

Preparation:
Collect simple newspaper articles to share.

Directions:
1. Have the children ask an older relative, such as a grandparent, to name an important event that occurred during his or her lifetime. (Or have the children choose an event from the list on this page.)
2. Using encyclopedias or other resources, have the children learn at least three facts about their chosen event.
3. Share short newspaper articles with the students. Then work together as a class to write a brief sample article.
4. Have the children write up their own newspaper articles about the events they've chosen, incorporating the facts they discovered.
5. Bind the stories together in a classroom book.

Note:
Younger children can dictate their stories or draw pictures of events.

Let children choose events from the following list:
1900s: First airplane flight took place in 1903.
1910s: World War I lasted from 1914-1918.
1920s: Regularly scheduled U.S. radio broadcasts occurred.
1930s: Screening of motion pictures with synchronized sound.
1940s: World War II ended in 1945.
1950s: NASA was established in 1958.
1960s: The U.S. landed astronauts on the moon.
1970s: Video games were mass produced.
1980s: Personal computers became popular.

Family Graphing

Children will use the number of people in their families to contribute to a classroom family graph.

Materials:
Large sheet of paper, crayons or markers

Preparation:
Create a grid to graph family members. The number of members can go across the bottom of the grid.

Directions:
1. Explain that the children will be graphing the number of people in their immediate families.
2. One at a time, let the children make a mark on the graph indicating the number of people in their families.
3. Discuss the results of the graph as a class.

Options:
• If possible, have the children find out how many members were in their grandparents' or great-grandparents' families. Graph these numbers and then compare with the modern family graphs. Children may be surprised to see how large many families were at the start of the 1900s.
• Graph extended families, including grandparents, aunts and uncles, cousins, and so on.

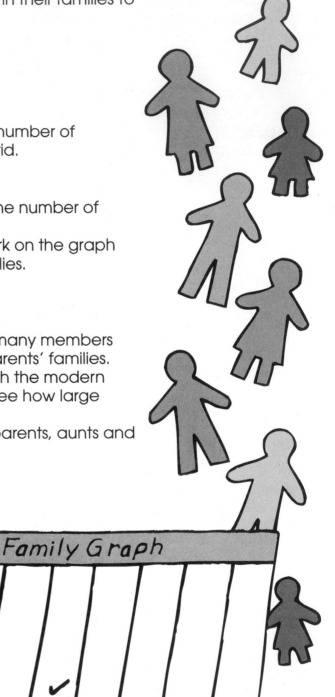

F Is for Families © 2002 Monday Morning Books

"It's All Relative" Spelling Bee

Materials:
Leaves (p. 28), Family Tree (p. 23), scissors, crayons or markers

Preparation:
1. Duplicate a copy of the spelling word patterns for each child and one for teacher use.
2. Cut the leaves apart and color as desired.
3. Enlarge the tree pattern and post on a bulletin board.

Directions:
1. Announce a date for a spelling "bee."
2. Divide the students into small groups. Have the children work together to learn the words. Let the children take the leaves home to study.
3. On the day of the spelling bee, put the leaves in a bag. Pull one leaf from the bag at a time and have a child spell the word on the leaf.
4. If the child spells the word correctly, he or she can post the leaf on the tree. If not, another child tries to spell the word.
5. Continue until each child has a chance to spell one word, and all of the leaves are posted on the tree.

Options:
• Use the blank leaves to make enough words for each child in the classroom to spell at least one. Or re-use words to let each child have a turn.
• White-out the given spelling words and write in other family-related words.

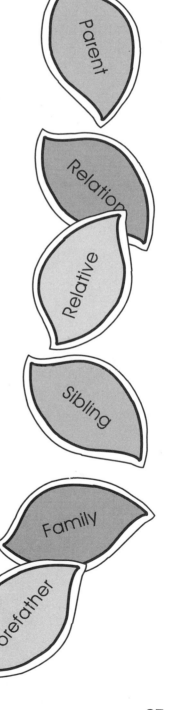

Leaves

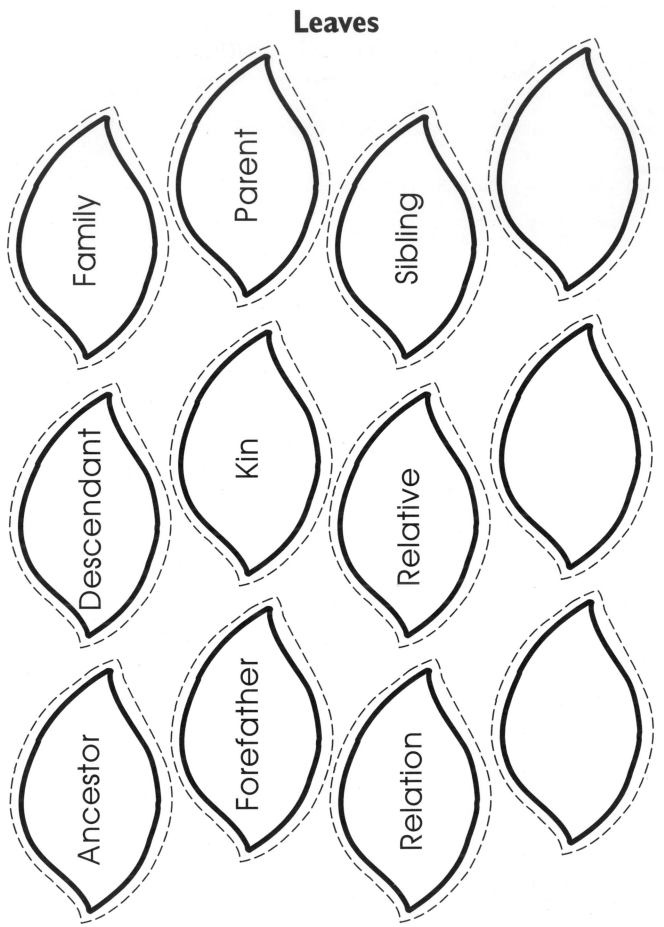

Family

Parent

Sibling

Descendant

Kin

Relative

Ancestor

Forefather

Relation

Old-Time Photos

Posing for pictures is an everyday occurrence now. However, in the early days of photography, taking pictures was very unusual!

Materials:
Photo patterns (p. 30), colored pencils

Preparation:
Duplicate the Photo Patterns for each child.

Directions:
1. Give each child a copy of the photo patterns.
2. If possible, show the children old-fashioned photographs, either from your own family or from a book.
3. In the ovals, have the children draw self-portraits or pictures of family members.
4. Provide colored pencils for children to use to "tint" the pictures.
5. Host a gallery opening in which the children's old-time photos are on display.

Options:
• Gather books with old-time photographs to place near the children's drawings.
• Have the children bring in photographs from home. They can cut out the faces in their photos and glue them to the photo patterns. (Let parents know that the photos will be used in an art project.)

Photo Patterns

Who Am I?

For this game, children will interact with each other and give each other clues as to which type of family member they are supposed to be.

Materials:
Family Members patterns (p. 32), scissors, tape

Preparation:
Duplicate the family patterns and cut them apart.
Make one for each child.

Directions:
1. Tape one pattern to each child's back. (Don't let the children see their own patterns.)
2. Have the children walk around the room and talk to each other. During their conversations, they will try to give subtle clues to each other as to which family member they're supposed to be. For example, one child might say, "I don't want to clean my room," to a child wearing a parent picture. Or "Stop taking my toys!" to a child wearing a sister picture.
3. Once a child has correctly guessed the pattern on his or her back, the child can sit down or help others with clues.

Options:
• Let children draw pictures of family members. Cut these out, label them, and use them as the patterns for the game.
• Help children to develop different clues ahead of time.

Family Members

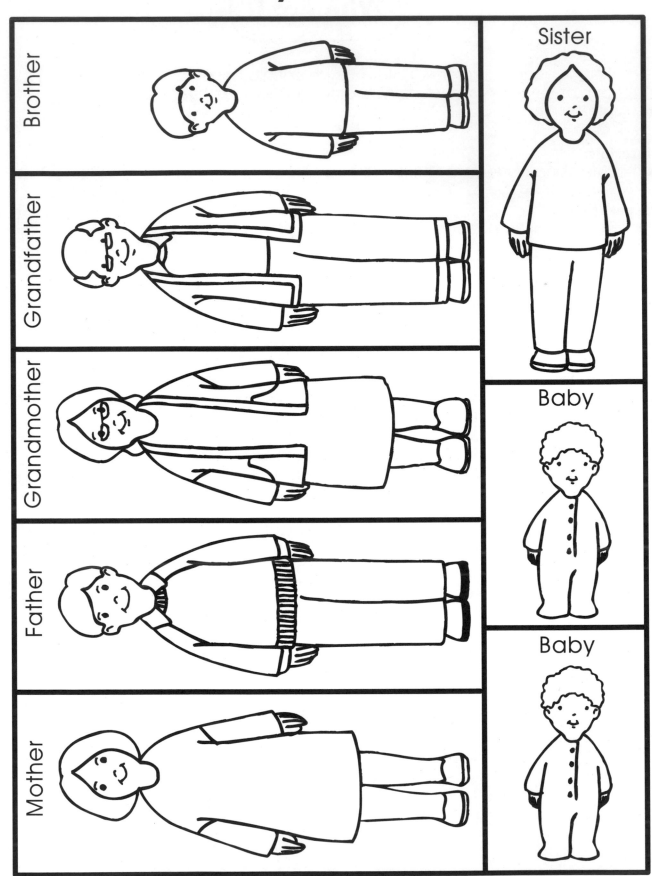

F Is for Families © 2002 Monday Morning Books

Family Tree Song

Family Tree
(to the tune of "Jingle Bells")

Grandmothers, grandfathers,
Aunts, and uncles, too,
Moms, and dads, and children,
Just like me and you,
Put them all together, in one big family.
All of your relations make up your family tree.

There are nieces and nephews,
Sisters, and brothers, too,
Your grandmas and grandpas
Related all to you!

The ones from long ago,
Started your family tree,
Ancestors you don't know
Began your family.

Oh, grandmothers, grandfathers,
Aunts, and uncles, too,
Moms, and dads, and children,
Just like me and you,
Put them all together, in one big family.
All of your relations make up your family tree.

Family Event Calendars

This activity allows children to keep track of the different events that are important to their families. The events could include holidays, as well as special family days.

Materials:
Calendar Pattern (p. 35), construction paper, scissors, crayons and markers, pens or pencils

Preparation:
Duplicate 12 Calendar Patterns for each child.

Directions:
1. Give each child a set of Calendar Patterns to decorate with crayons or markers. They can glue the patterns to colored construction paper for colorful borders.
2. Explain that the children will use the calendars to keep track of birthdays, anniversaries, and other events that are important to their families, such as Mother's Day, Father's Day, and Grandparents' Day. They should start by writing in their own birthdays on the calendars.
3. Let the children take their calendars home. Their relatives can help them fill in the calendars. Then the calendars can be posted in a place where their families can use them.

Option:
Have the children bring their filled-in calendars back to school to post on a "Special Days" bulletin board.

34

Calendar Pattern

Family Traditions

Children will be interested in learning how their classmates celebrate different events.

Materials:
Storybooks about traditions, crayons or markers, paper, pens or pencils

Preparation:
Gather storybooks that discuss different family traditions.

Directions:
1. Explain that the class will be working together to create a book about traditions. Tell the students that a tradition is a special way of doing something. For instance, one family's tradition might be to open one present the night before a birthday rather than waiting until the actual day. Another family might celebrate half-birthdays. Or a family might have one day each week set aside for family day.
2. Have the children write down a few sentences explaining a tradition that their family has. They should say how long their family has had this tradition.
3. Provide crayons and markers for the children to use to illustrate the tradition.

Definition:
According to *Webster's New World College Dictionary*, one definition of the word "tradition" is the handing down orally of stories, beliefs, and customs from generation to generation.

At our house we open one gift in the morning.

We have a scavenger hunt on our birthdays.

Go to the hall.

Look under the plant.

Close the mini blinds.

Go to page 72 in the Y encyclopedia.

Saturday night is our family night. We play games.

Family Fables

In this fun activity, children will be retelling famous fables and folk tales with their own families as the stars. Consider writing your own retold fable to share with the students as a way of starting this activity.

Materials:
Storybooks, paper, pens or pencils, crayons or markers

Preparation:
Gather a collection of famous fables or fairy tales, such as "Goldilocks and the Three Bears," "The Three Billy Goats Gruff," "Snow White and Seven Dwarfs," and so on.

Directions:
1. Read one of the books listed above. Or choose a book that includes the telling of a story within the story.
2. Explain that the children will be rewriting fables with their own family members as the stars. For instance, a child rewriting "The Three Billy Goats Gruff," might use his mother and father and himself in the place of the goats.
3. Have the children illustrate the stories and share them with their classmates.

Options:
• Bring books into the class that have stories within stories, such as *Tell Me a Trudy* or *Tell Me A Mitzi*, both by Lore Segal, or *The Three Sillies*.
• Instead of retelling a famous fable, the children can write their own.

How Many Presents?

This math activity can be used for different levels of mathematical study. For younger children, write a plus or minus sign in the balloon at the center of each equation. Write in a multiplication sign for older children.

Materials:
Presents Math (p. 39), pencils, crayons or markers

Preparation:
1. Fill in the missing signs (+, -, or x), then duplicate the Presents Math pages. Make one for each child.
2. Make an answer key for self-checking, if desired.

Directions:
1. Give each child a copy of the Presents Math.
2. Have the children do the problems. They count the gifts on the left of the balloon and then look at the numeral on the right side of the balloon. They then see whether they are doing an addition, subtraction, or multiplication problem. They draw the correct number in the balloon at the right of the equals sign.
3. Children can share their answers with the class. Or they can use the answer key for self-checking.

Options:
• For older children, pass out the Presents Math pages without any signs written in the middle balloons. Let the children make their own problems to test their friends. They can add a +, -, or x and then write the answers on the back. Have the children trade papers.
• To make the problems more difficult, add more gifts to the equations.

F Is for Families © 2002 Monday Morning Books

Presents Math

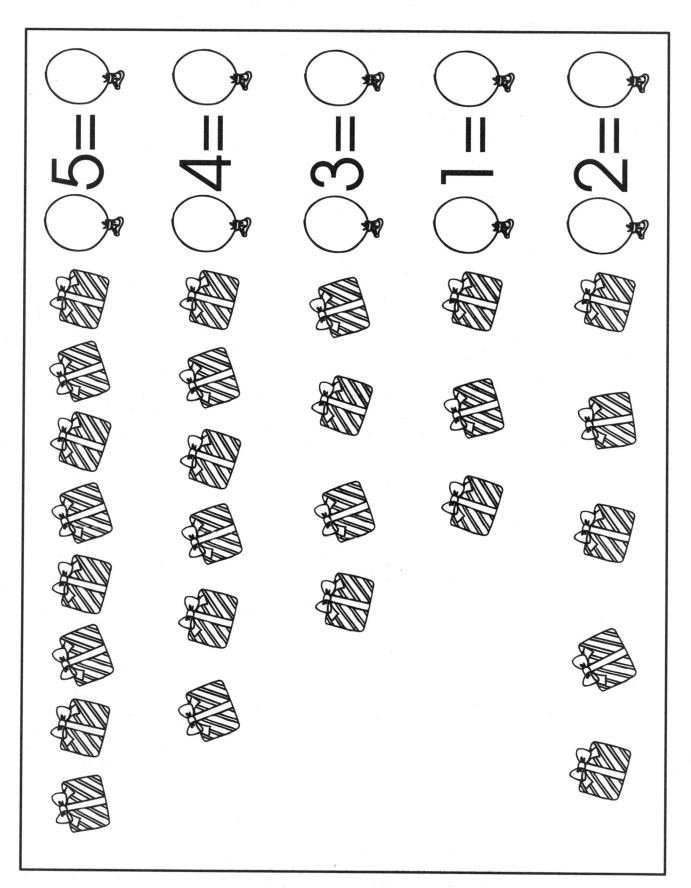

Family Traditions Spelling

Materials:
Candles (p. 41), Cake (p. 42), bag, construction paper, scissors, colored markers

Preparation:
1. Duplicate a copy of the Candles for each child and one for teacher use.
2. Cut one set of the Candles apart and color as desired.
3. Enlarge the Cake, color as desired, and post on the bulletin board.

Directions:
1. Announce a date for a spelling "bee."
2. Divide the students into small groups. Have the children work together to learn the words. Let the children take the Candles home to study.
3. On the day of the spelling bee, put the Candles in a bag. Pull one from the bag at a time and have a child spell the chosen word.
4. If the child spells the word correctly, he or she can post the Candle on the Cake. If not, another child tries to spell the word.
5. Continue until each child has a chance to spell one word, and all of the Candles are posted on the board.

Options:
• Use the blank Candles to make enough words for each child in the classroom to spell at least one. Or re-use words to let each child have a turn.
• White-out the given spelling words and write in other words.

F Is for Families © 2002 Monday Morning Books

Candles

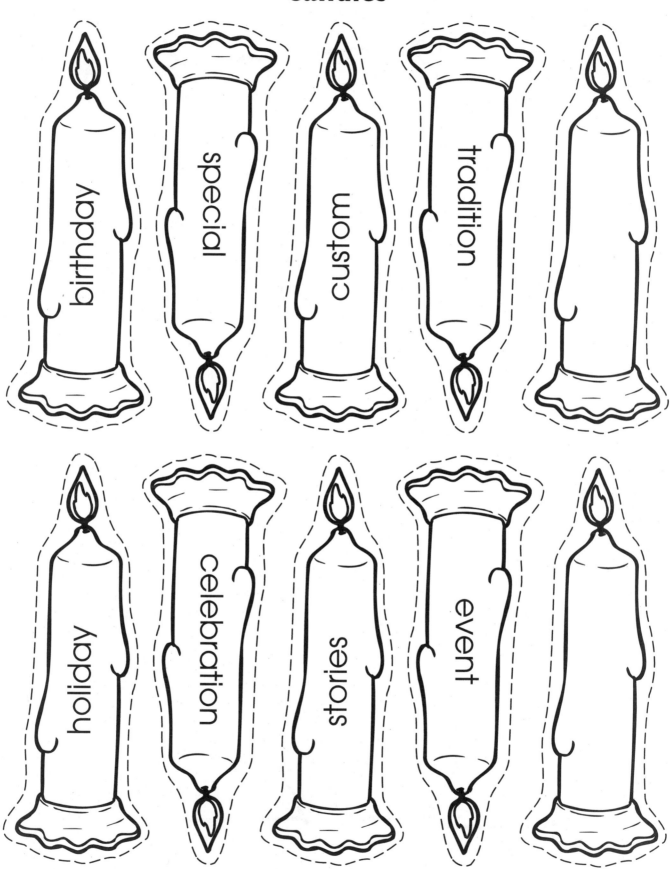

birthday

special

custom

tradition

holiday

celebration

stories

event

Cake

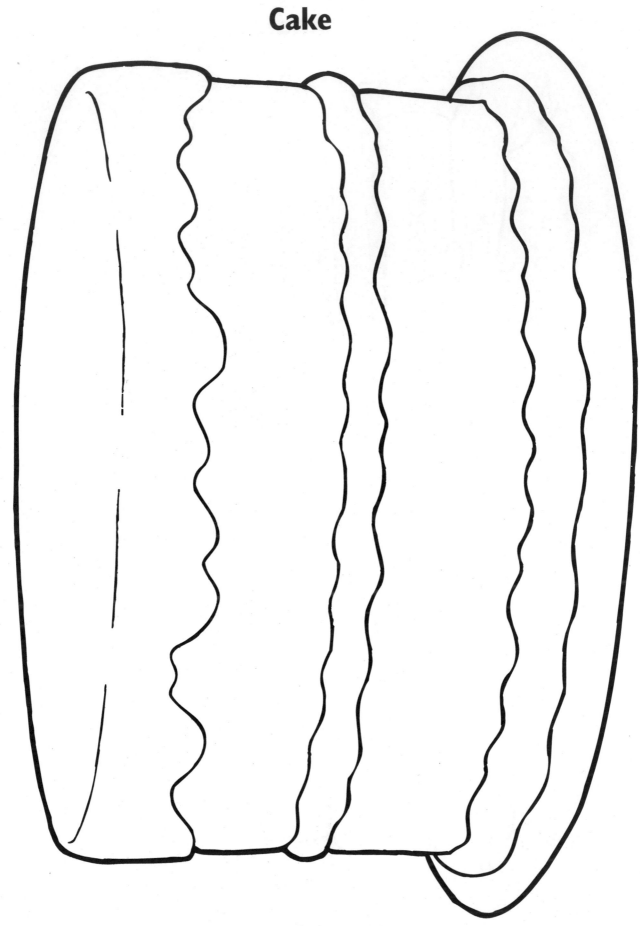

Creating Cards

Depending on the time of year that you do this activity, children can make Mother's Day, Father's Day, or Grandparents' Day cards. Or they can make cards for special birthdays, anniversaries, or other family events.

Materials:
Great Greeting Cards Patterns (p. 44), paper, scissors, glue, crayons or markers, glitter (optional)

Preparation:
Duplicate a copy of the Great Greeting Cards Patterns for each child.

Directions:
1. Have the children fold their papers in half, then in half again to create cards.
2. Children can use the Great Greeting Cards patterns, or make drawings of their own to cut out and glue to the cards.
3. Provide additional decorations, such as glitter and glue for children to use to make their cards extra-special.

Book Link:
• *Mr. Rabbit and the Lovely Present* by Charlotte Zolotow
In this sweet story, a rabbit helps a little girl find the perfect present for her mother.

Great Greeting Cards Patterns

Playing Piñata

Some families celebrate birthdays with a rousing tradition of trying to break the piñata. Children will work together to create one or several piñatas. Then they can work together to demolish the colorful creations!

Materials:
Flour, water, inflated balloons, shredded newspaper, tempera paint, paintbrushes, shallow tins (for paint and papier-mâché mix), crepe paper, glue, toy or candy prizes and tape (optional)

Preparation:
Mix the flour and water together to make a water paste.

Directions:
1. Demonstrate how to make a papier-mâché creation. Children will be working together in small groups. They will be layering shredded newspaper dipped in the flour-and-water paste and then placing the newspaper onto a balloon. Their goal is to completely cover the balloon.
2. When the balloons dry, children can use tempera paint or crepe paper to decorate their piñatas.
3. Either hang the piñatas in the room, or let the children take turns trying to break the piñatas with a stick. (They should be blindfolded while they attempt this.) If breaking piñatas, you might want to insert toys or candy into the piñatas ahead of time. (Cut a hole in the bottom of a dry piñata, fill with treats, then seal again with tape.)

Web Links:
http://www.pacificacademy.com/how_to_make_a_pinata.htm
http://www.web-holidays.com/demayo/pinata.htm

Celebration Songs

Hip, Hip, Hooray!
(to the tune of "Row, Row, Row, Your Boat")

Hip, hip, hip, hooray,
Today is your birthday!
Happily, happily, happily, happily
Celebrate your day!

Note: Fill in the correct age of the child, for instance, sing,
"It's your sixth birthday."

A New Birthday Song
(to the tune of "Jingle Bells")

Birthday cake, big balloons, pretty presents, too,
Today it is your birthday—a happy day to you!
Noisemakers, silly games,
Your friends all gather round
To sing a special birthday song,
Oh, what a pretty sound!

Today is your birthday.
Your friends all want to say,
We know you'll have great fun
On your very special day.

We hope that this whole year
Brings many times of joy.
We all wish you good cheer—
May you get a lot of toys!

Oh, birthday cake, big balloons,
Pretty presents, too,
Today it is your birthday—a happy day to you!
Noisemakers, silly games,
Your friends all gather round
To sing a special birthday song,
Oh, what a pretty sound!

F Is for Families © 2002 Monday Morning Books

Home for the Holidays

Around the world, families celebrate different holidays. Even the same holidays, such as April Fool's Day, are often celebrated in different ways. Use the Web sites listed below to find information about many different holidays around the world!

Materials:
Holiday Celebration patterns (p. 48), crayons or markers

Preparation:
Duplicate a copy of the Holiday Celebrations sheet for each child.

Directions:
1. Give each child a holiday sheet to color using crayons or markers.
2. Have the children share the sheets with their families. On the backs of the papers, have them write in (or illustrate) a special way that they celebrate one or more of the holidays with their families. Or the children can choose to write or draw something about a different holiday that is important to their families.
3. Let the children share their holiday celebrations with the rest of their classmates.

Holiday Web Sites:
http://www.web-holidays.com/holidays.htm
http://www.falcon.jmu.edu/~ramseyil/holidays.htm
http://www.holidays.net/
http://wfs.vub.ac.be/cis/festivals/
http://www.usis.usemb.se/Holidays/celebrate/April.htm

Holiday Celebrations

F Is for Families © 2002 Monday Morning Books

Time-Capsule Reports

In this activity, children research the way families lived a long time ago. Use the Ancient History Cards for research, or have the children work with encyclopedias and other resources. Each of the cards includes a picture of a dwelling from ancient times, as well as several items used by the culture.

Materials:
Ancient History Cards (p. 50), scissors, shoe box (one per group), drawing paper, crayons or markers

Preparation:
Duplicate the Ancient History Cards.

Directions:
1. Explain that the children, in groups, will be choosing a time period to research. They might choose pioneer, colonial, ancient Greek, or other periods. Their goal is to learn several facts about families who lived during their chosen time period.
2. Divide the children into small groups and provide Ancient History Cards or other resources for children to use to do research.
3. Have the children prepare time capsules that might have been put together by a family who lived in their chosen period. For instance, a colonial family might put a picture of a wagon wheel, a prairie schooner, and a team of oxen in the capsule. The children should draw pictures of items, cut them out, and place them in the shoe boxes.
4. Have the children share their time capsules with the rest of the class.

Book Link:
• *Little House on the Prairie* by Laura Ingalls Wilder

Ancient History Cards

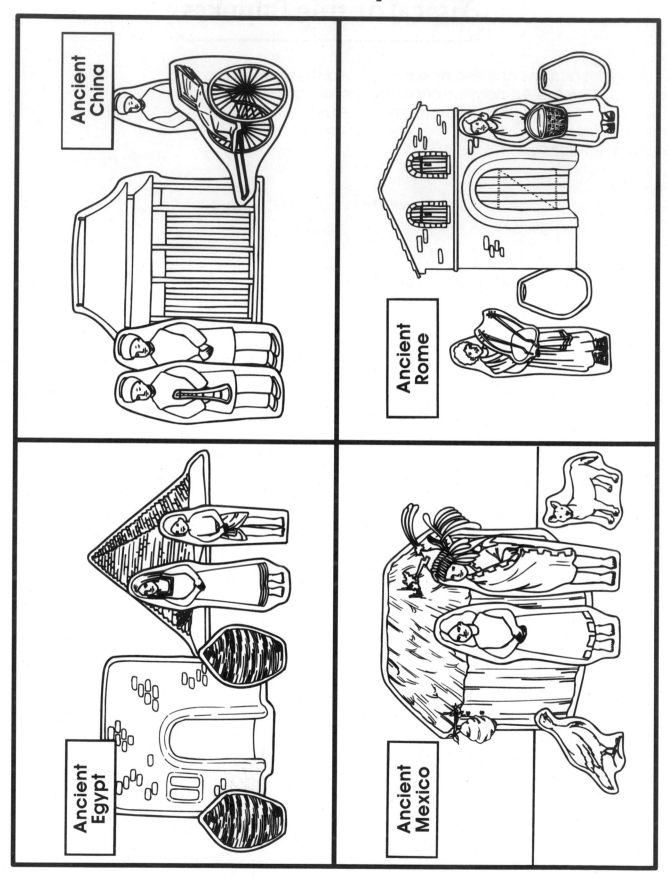

Ancient China

Ancient Rome

Ancient Egypt

Ancient Mexico

Postcards from the Past

In this activity, the children will pretend that they live long ago. They will write a postcard or letter to someone in the future (now) describing their family's lifestyle.

Materials:
Postcard Patterns (p. 52), books about families from long ago, paper, pens or pencils, crayons or markers

Preparation:
1. Gather together resource books about families.
2. Duplicate the Postcard Patterns.

Directions:
1. Have the children research a chosen time period. They can use the books or encyclopedias.
2. Provide the Postcard Patterns or rectangles of paper for the children to use to write postcards. If making the cards themselves, they can illustrate the backs with pictures.
3. Give each child a chance to share his or her postcard with the rest of the class.
4. Post the complete messages on a bulletin board near books about families from the past.

Book Link:
• *Turn of the Century* by Ellen Jackson (Charlesbridge, 1998). This creative and informative book provides information on the way that children lived in each century starting with the year 1000.

Dear Thomas,
We are traveling in our new Model-T automobile. The countryside is pretty. Mother and father said we should be in Chicago by next Thursday. I am looking forward to visiting another big city.
Wilma

Dear Lucy,
I am so excited. We will arrive in Houston on Friday. Father says we will be able to sleep in real beds again when we get there. I like traveling in the wagon but I don't like it when we have to sleep on the ground. There are many wild animals.
Melanie.

Dear Mary,
We arrived in the Oregon territory yesterday. The ride in the wagon was hard. We had to cross a river. It was exciting but very scary. Tomorrow we will go hunting for food. We hope to arrive in California in another three weeks.
Tammy

Greetings From Our Cross Country Drive

Greetings From the West

Postcard Patterns

Greetings From the West

Greetings From Our Cross Country Drive

F Is for Families © 2002 Monday Morning Books

How Many Schooners?

This prairie math activity can be used for different levels of mathematical study. For younger children, write a plus or minus sign the middle camp fire of each equation. Write in a multiplication sign for older children.

Materials:
Prairie Math (p. 54), pencils, crayons or markers

Preparation:
1. Fill in the missing signs (+, -, or x), then duplicate the Prairie Math pages. Make one for each child.
2. Make an answer key for self-checking, if desired.

Directions:
1. Give each child a copy of the Prairie Math.
2. Have the children do the problems. They count the schooners on the left of the campfire and then look at the numeral on the right side of the campfire. They then see whether they are doing an addition, subtraction, or multiplication problem. They write the correct numeral after the equals sign.
3. Children can share their answers with the class. Or they can use the answer key for self-checking.

Options:
• For older children, pass out the Prairie Math pages without any signs written in the campfires. Let the children make their own problems to test their friends. They can add a +, -, or x and then write the answers on the back. Have the children trade papers.
• To make the problems more difficult, add more schooners to the papers.

Prairie Math

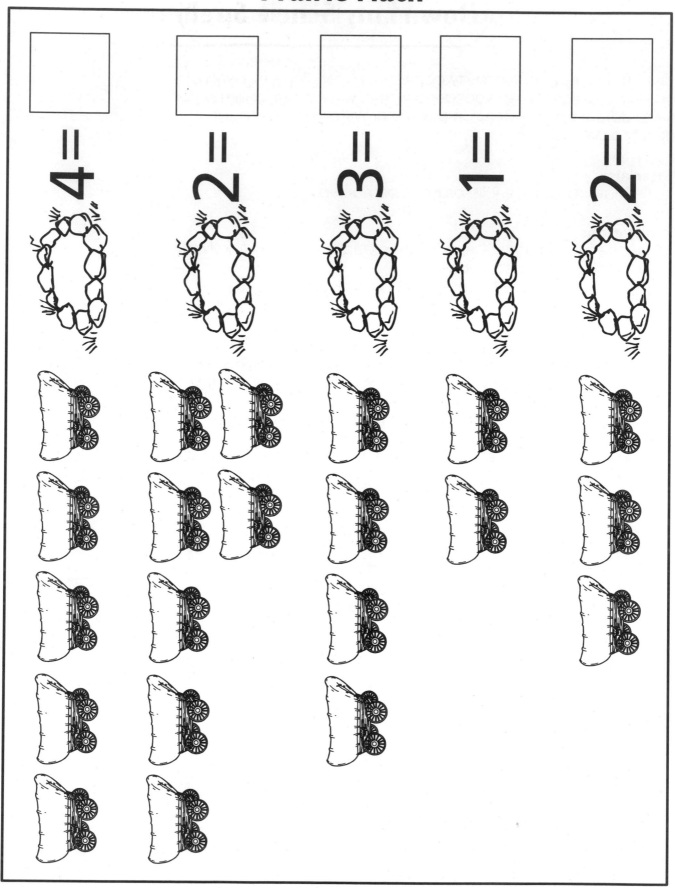

F Is for Families © 2002 Monday Morning Books

House on the Prairie Spelling

The words listed on these wagons are related to life during the pioneer times. For instance, many families lived in log cabins. When studying another era, choose other words that would have been important to families of the times.

Materials:
Prairie Schooners (p. 56), bag, construction paper, scissors, colored markers

Preparation:
1. Duplicate a copy of the Schooners for each child and one for teacher use.
2. Cut one set of the Schooners apart and color as desired.

Directions:
1. Announce a date for a spelling "bee."
2. Divide the students into small groups. Have the children work together to learn the words. Let the children take the schooners home to study.
3. On the day of the spelling bee, put the schooners in a bag. Pull one pattern from the bag at a time and have a child spell the word on the schooner.
4. If the child spells the word correctly, he or she can post the schooner on the bulletin board. If not, another child tries to spell the word.
5. Continue until each child has a chance to spell one word, and a wagon train covers the bulletin board.

Options:
• Use the blank schooners to make enough words for each child in the classroom to spell at least one. Or re-use words to let each child have a turn.
• White-out the words on the patterns and write in other spelling words.

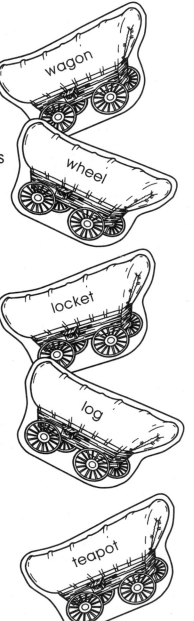

Prairie Schooners

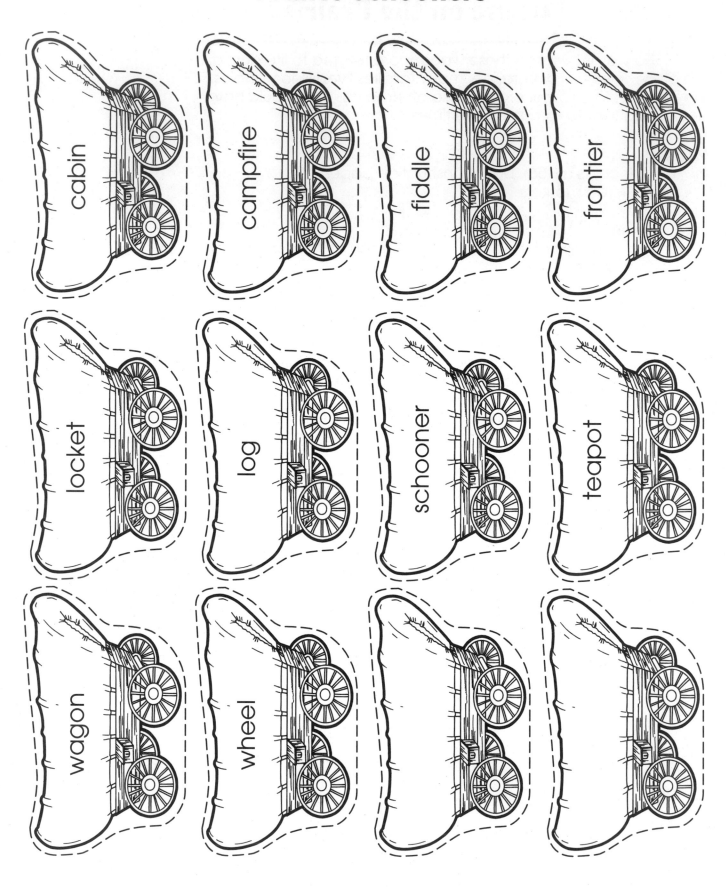

cabin

campfire

fiddle

frontier

locket

log

schooner

teapot

wagon

wheel

Lovely Lockets

Today, it's easy for people to carry pictures of their families with them. A hundred years ago, a photograph was more difficult to come by and treated as a special token.

Materials:
Heavy paper, scissors, crayons or markers, yarn, hole punch

Preparation:
Fold the paper in half and cut the circles on the fold, leaving an uncut hinge. (This is the same method used when making a Valentine heart.)

Directions:
1. Give each child a circle.
2. Have the children draw self-portraits or pictures of their families on the inside of the circles.
3. Children can decorate the front of the circle.
4. If a hole is punched in the lockets, children can thread through with a piece of yarn to make a necklace.
5. Lockets make creative gifts for family holidays, such as Mother's Day, Father's Day, or Grandparents' Day.

Options:
• Have the children bring photos from home to use in this activity.
• Duplicate the different Locket Patterns (p. 58) for use in this activity. Children can trace the patterns onto folded paper and cut out.

Locket Patterns

Who Wants to Be a Genealogist?

Children will challenge each other with multiple-choice questions to share what they know about families and history. Explain the term "genealogist" ahead of time.

Materials:
Quiz Questions (p. 60), scissors, index cards, pencils, resource books about families

Preparation:
None

Directions:
1. Explain the game. You will read off a question and four possible answers. Children who think they know the answer, will raise their hands. Choose one child to answer. If he or she is correct, let this child read the next question. If not, keep going until a child answers correctly.
2. Once the children understand the game, have each child create his or her own question with four possible answers. The children should write the question and answers on one side of an index card and the correct answer on the back. They can use information from this book, or from resource books about families. Be sure to explain that three of the answers should be incorrect and only one will be correct.
3. Gather all of the children's questions and continue with the quiz game. Or let the children quiz each other.

Options:
• Let the children have a chance to remove two incorrect answers.
• Allow children to confer with a friend about the correct answer.

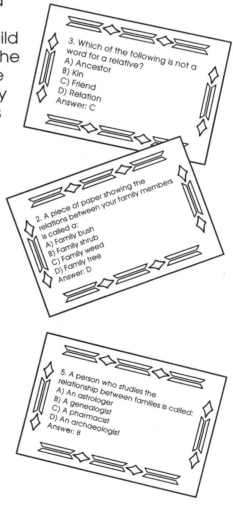

3. Which of the following is not a word for a relative?
A) Ancestor
B) Kin
C) Friend
D) Relation
Answer: C

2. A piece of paper showing the relations between your family members is called a:
A) Family bush
B) Family shrub
C) Family weed
D) Family tree
Answer: D

5. A person who studies the relationship between families is called:
A) An astrologer
B) A genealogist
C) A pharmacist
D) An archaeologist
Answer: B

Quiz Questions

1. If your mother had a brother he would be:
A) Your cousin
B) Your nephew
C) Your uncle
D) Your aunt
Answer: C

2. A piece of paper showing the relations between your family members is called a:
A) Family bush
B) Family shrub
C) Family weed
D) Family tree
Answer: D

3. Which of the following is not a word for a relative?
A) Ancestor
B) Kin
C) Friend
D) Relation
Answer: C

4. A special way that a family celebrates an important event is called:
A) A tradition
B) A contradiction
C) A radiation
D) A dictionary
Answer: A

5. A person who studies the relationship between families is called:
A) An astrologer
B) A genealogist
C) A pharmacist
D) An archaeologist
Answer: B

Family Songs

I'm Part of a Family
(to the tune of "I'm a Little Teapot")

I'm part of a family,
So are you.
Each one's different.
This is true.
When you get together
You can see
Special things in your family.

You Have Many Kin
(to the tune of "Do Your Ears Hang Low?")

You have many kin
In the family that you're in.
Folks related all to you,
Forefathers and mothers, too.
Yes, your ancestry,
Was the start of your family.
You have many kin!

Family Fun

Before television, families entertained themselves in various ways. Children will work together to create a mural that shows modern and old-fashioned ways that families have fun.

Materials:
Family Fun Sheet (p. 63), books about families in the past, butcher paper, tempera paint, paintbrushes, shallow tins for paint

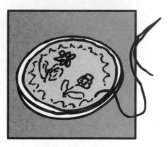

Preparation:
1. Gather together books about the past.
2. Duplicate a copy of the Family Fun Sheet for each child.

Directions:
1. As a class, research entertaining pastimes for families from long ago. (Or use the information below.)

2. Give each child a Family Fun Sheet to take home. Have the children talk with their families about their favorite ways to spend time together. They should fill in the sheets with their families. Challenge the children to try several of the pastimes from the past with their families.
3. When the children bring the filled-in sheets back to school, have them share the different ways that their families have fun together.

4. Have the children work together to create a cooperative mural showing ways that families have fun spending time together.

Pastimes of the Past:
• In the 1100s, a young lady might pass time by playing chess or embroidering.

• In the 1400s, children played hide and seek, made bubbles from soap, and played with shells and stones.
• In the 1600s, children played tenpins. Theaters were popular, and a play cost only one or two cents to see.
• In the 1800s, a family might pass the evening by singing.

F Is for Families © 2002 Monday Morning Books

Family Fun Sheet

My name is:

_____

My favorite way to have fun with my family is:

_____

_____

_____

_____

_____

_____

_____

We tried the following activities that children did long ago. (Circle each one you tried together as a family. If you tried other activities, draw a picture of each on the back of this page.):

  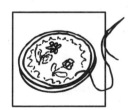

Name

HAS MASTERED

THE CONCEPT OF

FAMILY RELATIONSHIPS

AND IS AN HONORARY GENEALOGIST

HONORARY GENEALOGIST